Better Homes and Gardens®

AT THE ZOO

Hi! My name is Max.
I have some great projects
to show you—and they're all
about zoos! We're going
to have lots of fun making
them together.

FOREST HOUSE ®
School & Library Edition

Inside You'll Find...

Zoo Families 4

Take a look at the pictures. What's missing? Can you match the baby animals with their parents in the family pictures?

Clay Zoo Babies 6

Baby animals are very cute. Make your own family of animals out of homemade modeling clay. Let the shapes dry and then paint them.

Picture an Animal 8

Create an animal by arranging fabric shapes on a felt board. Then change them around to make a different animal picture.

Lions and Tigers 10

You'll have fun visiting the zoo with Max and and his best friend, Elliot. Look closely. Can you find the cats that are hidden in the picture?

Big Cat Mask 12

Grrrrrrr! Make a tiger, leopard, or lion mask using a paper plate. Decorate it with construction paper, crayons, and yarn.

Zoo Suit 14

It's fun to pretend you're a leopard or tiger. Just cut three holes out of a grocery bag, then paint the bag with spots or stripes. Put it on, and you're ready for a prowl through the jungle.

Home Sweet Zoo 16

Come on! Let's visit Max and his friends at the zoo. Here's a neat board game to play alone or with your family and friends.

Slippery Snakes 18

Let these creepy, crawly snakes made of gelatin slither their way to your tummy.

Zoo Cages 20

Create a foam-tray home for an animal that you have drawn or cut from an old magazine or coloring book.

Baked Elephant Ears 22

Shape pastry into large "elephant ears." Top with a cinnamon-sugar mixture for a quick-to-fix snack.

Monkeyshines 24

Oh, no! Some naughty monkeys have gotten loose at the zoo. Max and Elliot need your help to find them. Can you discover what sort of mischief they've done?

Monkeys in a Tree 26

Create your own troop of little monkeys from peanuts. Then hide them in a jungle tree that you make by tearing paper.

Monkey-Face Sandwich 28

This funny-looking sandwich tastes yummy! You'll go ape over its peanut butter and banana flavor.

Parents' Pages 30

We've filled this special section with more activities, suggestions of books to read aloud, and helpful project hints and tips.

Discover what's missing in these pictures.

Zoo Families

Max and his family had their picture taken together. Their friends at the zoo had their family pictures taken, too. Match the youngster with his or her family in each picture.

Who looks like me?

Look at the pictures of the youngsters below. Find their parents in the family pictures. In what ways do they look like their parents? Do you look like your mother or your father?

This inexpensive and versatile homemade clay offers hours of fun.

Clay Zoo Babies

Max likes to go to the zoo to see baby snakes, turtles, and bears. Have you ever seen a baby zoo animal? Which one is your favorite? Try to make it out of clay.

What you'll need...

- Tape
- Waxed paper
- Homemade Clay (see page 30)
- Water
- Fork
- Plastic wrap or foil
- Watercolors, tempera paint, or markers

1 Tape waxed paper to the work surface. To make a turtle, break off 5 small pieces of Homemade Clay about the size of a grape and 1 big piece the size of your fist. Roll each piece into a ball. For the turtle shell, flatten the biggest ball with the palm of your hand.

2 For the legs, place 2 small balls on one side of the turtle's shell. Place the other 2 balls on other side of the shell. Use the other small ball of clay for the head. Use a tiny piece of clay for the tail. Press the pieces onto the turtle's shell.

To make a pattern on the shell, press the tines of a fork on the dough (see photo).

3 Use the remaining clay to make bears, snakes, or other animals. Be sure to tightly wrap any unused clay in plastic wrap. Store it in the freezer or refrigerator.

Let the turtle dry overnight or until it hardens (see page 30). Decorate the turtle using watercolors.

This felt board puts a lid on clutter.

Picture an Animal

You can make many different animals using the same simple shapes. Move them around, and create a new animal each time.

What you'll need...

- 5½x8½-inch piece of felt to fit lid of box
- Cigar or school supply box
- Scissors
- White crafts glue
- 5½x8½-inch or larger piece of nonfusible, nonwoven interfacing
- Pen
- Crayons

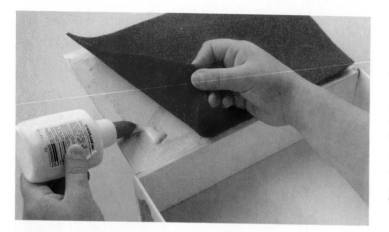

1 With adult help, fit the felt rectangle onto the inside of the cigar box lid. It may need to be trimmed a bit for a good fit. Make sure the felt clears the hinge, so the box will open and shut easily. Glue the felt in place (see photo). Press the felt until the glue starts to stick. Let the glue dry.

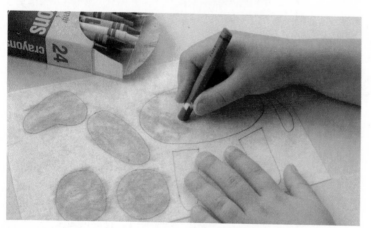

2 With adult help, use the picture on page 9 as a guide for making shapes on the interfacing. Use a pen to mark the interfacing. Decorate the shapes on the interfacing with crayons (see photo).

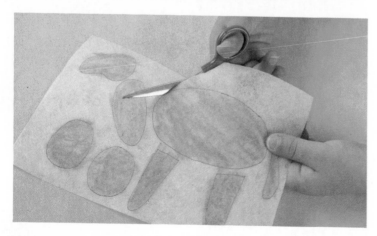

3 Cut out the shapes (see photo). See how many animals you can make by arranging the shapes on the felt inside the box lid.

When you are finished playing, store the shapes inside the box. You can take your box with you on trips and play with the shapes.

Simple Shapes

Scott made a rhinoceros (left). Then he rearranged his shapes and made a camel (below). It's fun to see all the animals you can make using simple shapes. Besides these shapes, try using triangles, squares, and rectangles.

Find the hidden cats.

Lions and Tigers

There are 6 big cats at the zoo hiding from Max. They're hard to find because their spots and stripes make them look like they are part of a tree, rock, or bush. Let's help Max find them.

Kinds of Big Cats

Leopard

Lion

Tiger

These fun-to-make cat masks offer a roaring good time.

Big Cat Mask

Do you or someone you know have a pet cat or a kitten? Zoos have some really big cats, such as lions, tigers, and leopards. Make a cat mask, and pretend you're a big cat.

What you'll need...

- Luncheon-size paper plate
- Scissors
- Pencil
- Seven 1x3-inch strips of paper
- White crafts glue
- Crayons
- 4 pipe cleaners
- Tape
- 2 pieces yarn or string, about 8 inches long

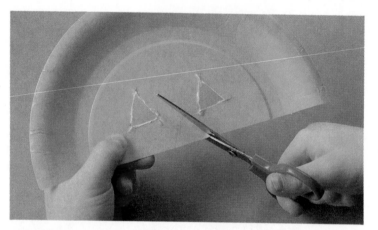

1 Cut the paper plate in half. With adult help, hold one of the paper-plate halves up to your face, and mark where to cut holes for your eyes. Cut out 2 triangles or circles for eyes (see photo). Hold the paper plate up to your face again, and mark on the front side of the plate where your nose is. Cut out a triangle-shaped piece.

2 Wrap one of the construction paper strips around a pencil to make it curl. Repeat until all of the strips have been curled. Glue the strips around the edge of the front side of the plate (see photo). Add more decorations to the mask with crayons and construction paper to make the type of cat you want.

3 For whiskers, take 2 pipe cleaners and fold them in half. Tape the folded pipe cleaners on one side of the nose. Do the same with the other 2 pipe cleaners. With adult help, use a pencil to poke holes in both sides of the mask next to where your ears will be. Push a piece of yarn through each hole, and tie a knot to hold.

13

Zoo Suit

Make a paper-bag shirt, and pretend you're any zoo animal you want to be. It's easy to paint on spots or stripes and make a tail so you look like your favorite animal.

What you'll need...

- 1 large plain paper grocery bag
- Scissors
- Wastebasket or box
- Newspapers
- Tempera paint in pie pan or other flat container
- Yarn or heavy string
- Tape

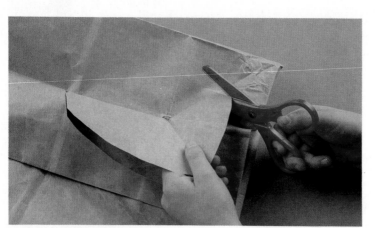

1 For shirt, with adult help, cut a slit down the front of the bag. Cut a hole in the bottom of the sack large enough to put your head through. Cut another hole on each side big enough to put your arms through (see photo). Open the bag and place it over the wastebasket. Place it on an area covered with newspapers.

2 Crumple ¼ sheet of newspaper. Dip it into tempera paint, and then touch it to the paper bag, pressing against the wastebasket to get a good print (see photo). Repeat until you have enough printed areas on the paper bag to look like spots for a leopard or giraffe, or stripes for a tiger or zebra. Let the bag dry.

3 To make a tail, cut 10 pieces of yarn, each about as long as from your elbow to your thumb. Hold the pieces together in one hand. Wrap the pieces with tape near one end to hold.
    Cut a small slit near the bottom edge of the back of your paper shirt. Push the taped end of the tail through the slit, and tape it to the inside (see photo).

roar roar Roar ROAR

Spend an afternoon at the zoo with this easy-to-learn board game.

Home Sweet Zoo

Come to the zoo to meet Max's animal friends. Start at the building with the flag. That's the admission gate. To play the game, follow the rules on page 17.

Start

Feed the giraffe some hay. Move 1 space.

Make a funny monkey face.

Grrrrrr! Roar like a lion. Move 5 spaces.

Rhino

A monkey grabbed your hat. Go back 1 space.

Share your popcorn. Move 2 spaces.

Turtles show you a shortcut. Move 4 spaces.

Hippo

The gorilla gives you a ride. Move 6 spaces.

Rest on a bench. Lose a turn.

Wiggle like a snake.

Zoo Game Rules

Be the first one to visit all the animals at the zoo—and that will make you the winner.

One player:
● Use different colors or sizes of buttons for markers. To begin, place 2 markers at the zoo's admission gate.
● Flip a penny. Move a marker 2 spaces if the penny lands on the head side and 1 space if it lands on the other side ("tails"). Flip again and move the other marker.
● Do what the spaces tell you to do. See which marker gets through the zoo first.

Two or more players:
● Have each player pick a marker. Take turns flipping the penny and moving the markers.

Count the bear cubs. Move 4 spaces.

A slide ride puts you ahead.

Have an ice-cream cone. Move 1 space.

Chirp, chirp! Make a bird sound.

QUACK!

Zebra

ELEPHANT CROSSING

Alligator

Meet a kangaroo. Jump ahead 2 spaces.

Tiger

Do an elephant walk.

Feed the seal a fish. Move 2 spaces.

You got wet! Lose 1 turn.

See Max feed the elephant.

PEANUTS

YOU WIN!

A wiggly gelatin snack that's fun to eat!

Slippery Snakes

Squeeze gelatin out of a hole snipped in a plastic bag to make these squiggly, jiggly snakes. Touch one, and see what happens!

What you'll need...

- 1½ cups apple juice
- Medium saucepan
- Hot pad
- One 3-ounce package any flavor of gelatin
- Wooden spoon
- Small mixing bowl
- 1 envelope unflavored gelatin
- 5 ice cubes
- 2 self-sealing plastic bags
- Baking sheet
- Foil or plastic wrap
- Scissors

1 Pour half of the apple juice into a saucepan. With adult help, heat the apple juice till boiling. Remove from heat. Place on hot pad. Carefully add flavored gelatin to hot apple juice. Using a spoon, stir till the specks of gelatin disappear.

Pour remaining apple juice into mixing bowl. Sprinkle it with unflavored gelatin.

2 Stir gelatin and juice in mixing bowl. Add it to hot apple juice. Add ice cubes. Stir until most of the ice cubes melt. Remove any unmelted ice cubes.

Refrigerate mixture till it is as thick as pudding, about 10 to 15 minutes. Have an adult help you put half of the apple gelatin into each plastic bag. Close each bag and seal.

3 Cover the baking sheet with foil. Cut about ¼ inch off one corner of the bag. Hold the bag over the baking sheet.

To make snakes, slowly move your hand while gently squeezing the bag so the gelatin oozes out (see photo). Repeat with remaining mixture. Put the snakes in the refrigerator. Chill about 2 hours.

Fun Food

Kids delight in using their fingers to eat this squiggly treat. Brettney (left), one of our kid-testers, has her colorful, wriggly snake firmly in hand.

Strawberry, raspberry, and cherry flavors give you red snakes, lemon makes yellow, and lime turns out green. Guess what color orange makes.

Use this simple weaving technique to make a clever cage.

Zoo Cages

Turn a foam tray into an animal-cage picture frame to show off pictures of your favorite animal.

What you'll need...

- Pictures of animals from old magazines or coloring books
- Scissors
- White crafts glue
- Plastic-foam tray
- 1 piece of yarn or string (about 36 inches long)
- Tape

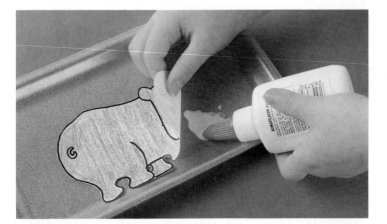

1 Find a picture of your favorite zoo animal in a magazine or coloring book, or draw one of your own. Use scissors to cut it out. Glue the picture in the center of the foam tray (see photo).

2 With your scissors, make cuts about 1 inch apart along one side of the tray. Cut just through the edge of the tray, about ½ inch. Turn the tray around and make more cuts on the side across from the ones you just made (see photo). Tape 1 end of the yarn on the back of the tray near one corner.

3 Guide the yarn into the first cut. Wrap it across the picture into the cut across from the first one (see photo). Press the yarn in, wrap it around the back of the tray. Repeat until all the cuts are filled with yarn. When you get to the end, cut the yarn, leaving about a 2-inch piece. Tape the extra yarn to the back of the tray.

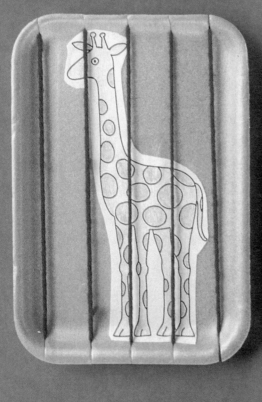

Piecrust mix makes this home-baked snack easy.

Baked Elephant Ears

How do you eat an elephant? One bite at a time! Start with this snack that's shaped like an elephant ear.

What you'll need...

- 1 stick of piecrust mix
- Medium mixing bowl
- Measuring spoons
- Hot water

- Fork
- Wood board
- All-purpose flour
- Baking sheet

- 2 tablespoons sugar
- 2 teaspoons ground cinnamon
- Shaker or spoon

1 With adult help, break piecrust into little pieces in the bowl. Add 3 tablespoons of hot water. Mix with a fork till the dough sticks together.

2 Sprinkle the wood board with flour. Pat your hands with flour. Form the dough into a big ball on the board.
Divide the dough into 4 parts. Form each part into a ball.
To make elephant ears, use your whole hand to flatten each ball (see photo). Press hard so the dough gets thinner. It should be about ¼ inch thick.

3 Place each piece of dough onto an ungreased baking sheet. Mix together sugar and cinnamon. Place in shaker. Sprinkle the cinnamon-sugar topping on your elephant ears. Be careful not to get the sugar on the baking sheet.
    With adult help, bake at 350° for 20 minutes or till golden brown. Cool. Makes 4.

Big Treats

One of our kid-testers couldn't wait to draw a picture of an elephant using the tasty elephant ears. You, too, can draw one, using crayons.

For decoration, you can use colored sugar, chocolate sprinkles, nonpareils, or frosting instead of cinnamon and sugar.

Help straighten out the topsy-turvy zoo.

Monkeyshines

Somehow some mischievous monkeys have gotten things all mixed up at the zoo. Can you point to the 5 things that are wrong with the picture?

Torn-paper artwork makes a unique and surprising project.

Monkeys in a Tree

Hey, look! Do you see what's in the tree? Little monkeys made from peanuts are climbing on the branches. Create your own troop of monkeys to play in a jungle picture.

What you'll need...

- 1 piece of construction paper
- Tree Parts (see tip on page 27)
- White crafts glue
- Peanuts in the shell
- Crayons or markers
- Pieces of yarn or string, about 2 inches long

1 Turn the piece of construction paper so the longest side is closest to you. Glue the tree trunk on the paper. Glue the grass to cover the bottom of the tree trunk (see photo). To make a branch, fold a green paper strip in half. Glue the folded end on top of the tree trunk (see photo, page 27). Glue about 10 branches on your tree.

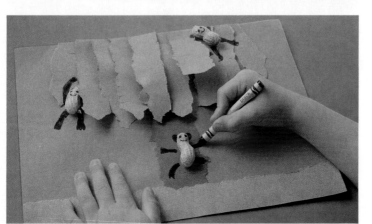

2 For the monkey's body, put glue on the paper and place a peanut in the shell on it. Use crayons to draw a face, legs, and arms (see photo).

3 To make a monkey's tail, put glue in the shape of a tail on the paper where the tail should be (see photo). Lay a piece of yarn on the glue. Let dry.

Tree Parts

Here are some tips for making the Monkeys in a Tree project:

● For the tree trunk, tear a strip of brown paper.
● For grass, tear a strip of green paper.
● For branches, tear about 10 strips of green paper.

27

Children enjoy making these delicious sandwiches.

Monkey-Face Sandwich

Does a monkey face make you giggle? This tasty sandwich will put a smile on your face before and after you eat it.

What you'll need...

- 4 slices thinly sliced, firm-textured whole wheat or white bread
- Cutting board
- 1 empty 8-ounce can or 1 empty 3-inch-diameter can or cutter
- Table knife
- Sandwich filling (see recipes on page 32)
- Raisins
- Plate

1 Lay a slice of bread on a cutting board. Press the can into the center of 1 slice of bread (see photo). Be sure to save the bread crusts. Repeat with remaining bread.

2 With a knife, spread the sandwich filling on 2 of the bread circles. Top with the 2 remaining bread circles. To make ears, use the pieces of bread crusts. Make eyes, noses, and mouths with raisins (see photo). To make them stick to the bread, put a little sandwich filling on the raisins. Makes 2 monkey faces.

Making Faces

Instead of using raisins, try nuts, cereal, or small pieces of carrot, celery, or fruit.

Use sandwich filling or peanut butter as the "glue" to hold the face decorations in place.

Parents' Pages

We've filled this special section with more activities, recipes, reading suggestions, hints we learned from our kid-testers, and many other helpful tips.

Zoo Families

See pages 4 and 5

Observing animals at the zoo is an enlightening experience for children and adults. Even if you can't visit a zoo, you can look at pictures and read to your children about animals. They'll love to talk and learn about animals.
● Reading suggestions:
Zoo by Gail Gibbons
Wild Animals in America
   by Hope Ryden

Clay Zoo Babies

See pages 6 and 7

The creations your children mold with Homemade Clay may take from a few hours to a day to air-dry. To speed drying, place the items on a baking sheet in a 300° oven for 30 minutes. Shut off oven and let cool for 1 hour. Continue to air-dry until the items harden.

Homemade Clay

   1 cup cornstarch
   1 1-pound box baking soda
1½ cups water

● In a large saucepan, mix cornstarch and baking soda together. Gradually add water. Cook and stir the mixture occasionally over low heat. The mixture will get bubbly, then thicken. Stir constantly until the mixture forms a ball.
● Remove from heat, and turn clay out onto plastic wrap or foil. It will thicken more after removing from the heat. It will be cool enough to handle within a few minutes. Use to make Clay Zoo Babies. Tightly wrap and refrigerate or freeze unused clay. Thaw frozen clay at room temperature and, if necessary, knead before using.

Clay Ornaments

Make teddy bear ornaments that smell good by adding about 2 tablespoons of ground cinnamon to half of the Homemade Clay recipe. Knead in more cinnamon, a tablespoon at a time, till bears are desired color.

Let your children roll out the clay to about ¼-inch thickness. Use cookie cutters to make shapes. Poke a hole for a hanger with a toothpick.

Picture an Animal

See pages 8 and 9

The children who helped us test this project liked using the nonwoven, nonfusible interfacing. It was easy to cut and decorate with crayons.

If you want, use felt instead of the interfacing. This option eliminates having to color the pieces. Cover the lid of the box with sandpaper. Glue or use double-faced tape to hold.

Lions and Tigers

See pages 10 and 11

Help your children learn about three types of big cats. Here are some interesting facts.
● Baby leopards look like ordinary domestic cats when they're first born. They have reddish brown coats with dark spots, but their coats turn to a smooth white splashed with black by the time they are grown.
● Tigers have loose skin and soft, tan-colored fur with black striped markings. Their ears are rounded.
● Lions have light golden coats with spots, which vary greatly from one "pride," or lion family, to another. Only male lions grow manes.

30

Big Cat Mask

See pages 12 and 13

Lions and tigers are favorites of zoo visitors of all ages. And children especially like zoo cats. Here's a chance for children to use their imagination to make cat masks.

You can use the same idea for making other masks for Halloween. Instead of curling construction paper, make paper feathers or hair.
● Reading suggestions:
Charles Tiger
    by Siobham Dodds
Zella, Zack, and Zodiac
    by Bill Peet

Zoo Suit

See pages 14 and 15

The newspaper printing technique used in this project makes great jungle camouflage. Your jungle explorer can make a safari shirt. Use green, brown, black, and tan paint.
● Reading suggestions:
1 Hunter by Pat Hutchins
Zoo by Jan Pienkowski
Dear Zoo by Rod Campbell

Home Sweet Zoo

See pages 16 and 17

Board games are entertaining, and they also can help your children practice skills needed for reading and math. This simple game helps children practice counting and reading readiness.

Slippery Snakes

See pages 18 and 19

Our kid-testers reacted with lots of giggles when they made these wiggly gelatin snakes.

For snakes with even more squiggle, use a cookie press to squeeze out zigzag snakes.

Fit the cookie press with a round tip. Fill with about half of the slightly thickened gelatin. Force the gelatin through the cookie press while slowly moving the cookie press back and forth in a zigzag motion.

Finished gelatin snakes need to be refrigerated. To keep finished snakes firm while serving, place them on a plate over a tray of ice cubes.

Zoo Cages

See pages 20 and 21

Here's a simplified form of weaving that most children can do on their own or with just a little adult help. This project uses a wrapping-type technique that our kid-testers quickly mastered.

Baked Elephant Ears

See pages 22 and 23

Have you ever had leftover pie-crust dough with cinnamon and sugar? With the convenience of ready-to-use pie-crust sticks, your children don't have to wait until you bake a pie to enjoy the cinnamon-spiced treat. These elephant ears are a variation of this familiar cinnamon snack and reminiscent of the pastry treat enjoyed by many people at fairs and festivals.

● Reading suggestions:
The Elephant and the Bad Baby
    by Elfrida Vipont
17 Kings and 42 Elephants
    by Margaret Mahy

Visit a Zoo

Many zoos have special programs and activities for children that will enhance their visit. There are many hands-on programs where children get to see some zoo animals up close or touch them.

Most larger zoos have education departments that conduct these programs for families and groups. Some have newsletters to publicize upcoming programs and events. Contact the zoo before your next visit to see what it has to offer.

Monkeyshines

See pages 24 and 25

You can play a fun game with your children that will help them develop listening skills and teach them to follow directions. Play Simon Says, but substitute the phrase "Monkey says." Have your children mimic your actions when you precede them with the phrase "Monkey says."

● Reading suggestion: *Curious George at the Zoo* by Margret Rey

Monkeys in a Tree

See pages 26 and 27

You and your children can use just the peanut shells in this project. That way, you can enjoy eating the peanuts. Remove the peanut shell with care, and glue it to the paper.

Snowman Sandwich

Create a snowman using different sizes of cans to cut the body out of white bread, and a knife to cut out a hat. Fill with sandwich filling, and arrange on a plate. Decorate with vegetables, raisins, dried fruit, or candy.

Monkey-Face Sandwich

See pages 28 and 29

Most kids love peanut butter. When stirred together with pineapple, banana, and carrot, it becomes a tasty sandwich filling for the Monkey-Face Sandwich. Or, try Tropical Strawberry filling that combines pineapple, banana, and coconut with strawberry-flavored, soft-style cream cheese.

When making either filling, save the pineapple can for cutting bread for the sandwich.

A round piece of bread also can be a lion's face, a smiling sun, or a snowman (see Snowman Sandwich, above). Or let your children use their imaginations to create their own special sandwiches.

Monkey's Delight

¼ cup peanut butter
2 tablespoons soft-style cream cheese
2 tablespoons milk
2 tablespoons crushed pineapple, undrained
1 tablespoon shredded carrot
2 tablespoons banana, chopped

● In a small bowl combine the peanut butter, cream cheese, and milk. Stir till well mixed. Stir in pineapple, carrot, and banana.
● Makes about ½ cup of filling or enough for 2 sandwiches.

Tropical Strawberry Filling

¼ cup strawberry-flavored, soft-style cream cheese
2 tablespoons crushed pineapple, undrained
2 tablespoons banana, chopped
1 tablespoon coconut

● In a small bowl combine the cream cheese and pineapple. Stir till well mixed. Stir in banana and coconut.
● Makes ½ cup of filling or enough for 2 sandwiches.

BETTER HOMES AND GARDENS® BOOKS
Editor: Gerald M. Knox
Art Director: Ernest Shelton
Managing Editor: David A. Kirchner
Department Head, Food and Family Life: Sharyl Heiken

AT THE ZOO
Editors: Sandra Granseth and Heather M. Hephner
Graphic Designers: Harjis Priekulis and Linda Ford Vermie
Editorial Project Manager: Angela K. Renkoski
Contributing Illustrator: Buck Jones
Contributing Photographer: Scott Little
Project Consultant: Marilyn Jean Giese

Have BETTER HOMES AND GARDENS®
magazine delivered to your door.
For information, write to:
ROBERT AUSTIN
P.O. BOX 4536
DES MOINES, IA 50336